HOT WITH THE BAD THINGS

A LYRIC

HOT

WITH THE

BAD

THINGS

LUCIA LoTEMPIO

Alice James Books

FARMINGTON, MAINE

alicejamesbooks.org

10 9 8 7 6 5 4 3 2 1

Alice James Books are published by Alice James Poetry Cooperative, Inc., an affiliate of the University of Maine at Farmington.

Alice James Books
114 Prescott Street
Farmington, ME 04938
www.alicejamesbooks.org

Library of Congress Cataloging-in-Publication Data

Names: LoTempio, Lucia, 1993- author.
Title: Hot with the bad things / Lucia LoTempio.
Description: [Farmington] : Alice James Books, [2020]
Identifiers: LCCN 2019044680 (print) | LCCN 2019044681 (ebook) | ISBN
    9781948579094 (paperback) | ISBN 9781948579650 (ebook)
Subjects: LCSH: Women--Violence against--Poetry. | LCGFT: Poetry.
Classification: LCC PS3612.O7747 H68 2020 (print) | LCC PS3612.O7747
    (ebook) | DDC 811/.6--dc23
LC record available at https://lccn.loc.gov/2019044680
LC ebook record available at https://lccn.loc.gov/2019044681

Alice James Books gratefully acknowledges support from individual donors, private foundations, the University of Maine at Farmington, the National Endowment for the Arts, and the Amazon Literary Partnership.

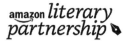

Cover art: Photo of woman by freestock.org on Unsplash. Texture by Wesley Tingey on Unsplash.
The emoji images in this work are licensed under Creative Commons (Attribution 3.0 Unported). Attributions: 1. "Heart, like, love, twitter icon" by Vectto, iconfinder.com/icons/2239656; 2. "Emoji, facebook, sad emoji, sad face icon" by Vectto, iconfinder.com/icons/2239885; 3. "Forgive, ied, muslim, peace, salam icon" by majnun studio, iconfinder.com/icons/4257758; 4. "Bible, book, chritian, cross icon" by Alpár-Etele Méder, iconfinder.com/icons/3030358.

for the girl I was and the women who know her

we might think of it as a shadow, but, in truth, the body is red.
BETH BACHMANN

In one sense it is a room I can never leave, perhaps dreadful for that. At the same time, a place composed entirely of entries. *Is it not astonishing, entry.*
ANNE CARSON

The man says, *Alone on a bus? That's how a horror movie starts.* But it feels more imaginable, tomorrow rather than a screen.

I should be a singed cauterization; removal to pin down this red. Hiding behind the poem is always another poem. And in that one, less blood. Or, a red more seeable and deserved. I don't know what I deserve anymore. And it's hard to know when everyone tells me I love myself. And I do. Really.

My friend got on the bus and the driver pleaded, *Oh honey, I'd love to see your face.* She tells me this belongs in a poem, but I don't think here is what she meant. The man on TV said, *Violence requires no imagination—anyone can shoot a gun.* But if the end of the barrel is the furthest distance he could imagine, I'm just not sure.

Listen: if nothing goes to plan, imagine it as bad as possible.

I kept waking after the moment of plunge. Smell thick warm humid dark. A knife to raise on the floor. A quick reach.

It was after the flood of posts—the man murdered the girl and her new lover. I was just a few months gone. I posted a picture too, a sunset posing as sunrise. Red hearts like playing cards.

As if I can play this mirror game. As if she could light through me. As if I am at the quiet swirling center.

Here, it opens with a metal snap. It is teeth put in a swinging hand. Puncture, closeness. In any case, some blood moves in something.

If telling a story is the mark of victory, what does that make me? Maybe power is like language—hard to nail down and relentless; smiling at a man who is waving to someone behind you.

When I write about the girl, I don't know a way that isn't obliteration.

The heart is flexible—pure creamed flesh if it flushed out all its blood.

As if I could touch her. And then? There are so many things a touch can be.

[Status Update Upstate]

I go back every few years. Nice kid, aw, he was
cute. Cold bloody killer. Anyone know her? No
girl is worth this and I know some perfect tens.
You know what we need? Knife control. I'm the
guy who's prepared, shoots bad guys when bad
things happen. Geneseo a sleepy town? Wake up
people. Clean your actions rid your mind of evil

If I'm at the wheel of this semitruck, I'm not opening onto a long stretch of highway—I'm not careening into a meticulously laid brick wall.

I'm a fever with the girl. I'm a fever with the things the man did to her.

In Geneseo there's a tree smacked with lightning, made lopsided like a children's book. Splinter sanded down by years of snow; vibration charted like an echo.

Here, a circle bright like lightning, but not blinking. Here, a circle begins at a weapon and can be penetrated.

A baby new to speech has every object named *this*. Green leaves white with sun, *this*. Red wrapper crinkling, *this*. My ring with the big chip, *this*. Her nose, *this*. Points and is satisfied.

I have tried to unclasp utterance from the dull edge of the girl's finger.

My capacity for imaging a violence flexes like a membrane. Like a girl. I would call it red.

When a girl is killed   When we say
her murderer as if it's a sweet
slow burn of possession   When the girl
was killed in Geneseo   When her ex
killed her   When the man killed her
When he stabbed her   When he killed
her lover   When he killed a man   When he
killed himself   When
at the memorial   When they don't
mention her   When iced
with blame   When a girl learns   When to keep
herself safe   When it's a matter of yelling *Fire*
not *Help me*   not *Rape*   not *Run*

[Status Update Upstate]

Thank you. It's difficult to process so much grief, confusion, and anger. ♡ Irrelevant. Broken hearts alone don't drive people. Excuses. Not the first time. I feel distraught over nonsensical posts about words we should or should not use. How about maddening. *rolls eyes* If you're totally bent on murder/suicide...do the suicide FIRST. Nope, no woman. I don't know what to say. Only love can do that.

In the bad dream I'm in the room.

In the bad dream the knife is infinite and repeating.

In the bad dream the knife is an instance of his body, another thing to go in and out.

In the bad dream I'm not her but I am watching.

In the bad dream why am I watching

After I heard about the murder, I began to write about the man I loved and what came next. Not a line but a loop.

I loved a man. I loved ●. I don't know how else to begin. I want to say I was a shadow. I want memory blotted out like a blank space.

Imagine a boundary rewired; to reach back and talk to myself. I'd say: *Lucia, you weren't full, but filling*. With what? A truth unknown and dreaded. Grasp for a word and not reach it; feel as if for silk in the empty valleys between fingers.

A friend once said we're just memories of each other until face-to-face. Well then I'm just a memory to me. Shuffle of you, I, our, untouchable and touching.

I'd say:

● was so angry after he raped you in your bed—said you weren't aroused at the angles of his body. Cross-legged, your hand to him without asterisk. Betrayal harsh and red in places—how could you? Open like the bowel of a rusted-out car hood, guide ● inside as if he wasn't the one holding the matches.

You ran up cardiac hill, raced ● so hard you threw up. The body works hard to forget—when a place is just valley, it's a lesson for lungs. And everything is apocalyptic if you pant hard enough.

Hill teemed with violence. Branch like a paw severed at the wrist. Shit as a spilled-out organ swarming green with flies. Rows of mailbox flags, hinged knives in red.

I'm sure you passed so many women, but you did not see one of them. The girl, years before the man murdered her, she helped you vacuum up a broken light bulb. Tingling shards on a coarse, matted carpet. Crush of metal, dust—glass so fine it went white. I don't remember her face at all. I'm looking for a word. Once a man took you behind one of those little mauve houses and you tasted another woman on him after he pushed you down to the snow.

And I went up the hill to class   And I had a body
And I had my body   And I had a whole
hike   And I was out of breath   And I panted
as if a man touched me   And I was on my knees
going up the stairs   And white bunnies
of dust stuck to me   And what stuck to me
was the smell of another hole   And I took
an apple   And I rested it in me   And I rested
And it was a round red in the light   And bright
And from underneath the man I loved
held me down   And pulled himself a slice
And the swift glare and ping of a pocketknife

You worked at Mia's—drank the weekend shift Labatts and Franzia and Malibu and the older girls made sangria with loganberry and Sprite and the cook took you out back to shotgun beers because you were cute in a sweet mouse way. When the owner told you to stir powdered sugar and milk until it was like a certain kind of fluid, you looked down.

Some backroom shift you were so drunk you got this wonderful bruise slipping on greased steps for storeroom hot sauce—lasted two weeks, ass a whole galaxy. Took a picture, sent it to ●. He liked that. Gave you a bracelet to rip the turquoise out of it. Gave him a knife with the handle made of goat bone. Kept in a drawer he opened in the morning.

Once, you vomited over a bed into a fold of blanket and some man kept fucking. Soon you realized how easy a man won't ask—and if you do slip away, how lucky to step off his stoop.

After the girl's ex-boyfriend killed her, the reporters said "Geneseo bar district"—there's just the one street. Main Street. After a few pitchers, you vomited on the flower shop stoop—first flat opening where sometimes the lights wouldn't turn on when you went under at night. It was fine. The place was so small. A roommate, probably Eliza, would keep the door unlocked. You'd place tips on the desk without coins touching.

If I take some
sand with me   I've left
a mark   If lamb
for slaughter then I'm not
a meal   If I'm tired
of decisions   If I'm not the center
of a round target   If ● finds
out he'll   If I hadn't
tied up my naked body   If
—yes—when   If he hasn't
forgotten   If he has
someone else   If in
a sand trap squirming

After sex, all sweat, a man laid out how to unsheathe a buck. Pointed on your thigh where to penetrate a fleshy doe. I don't want to be milking it. You felt his hand on the flank of your lean body, the prickle of where hair used to be, and I can remember it so bright and yellow and humid through the slotted drapes.

Eliza waiting, got smiley potatoes at brunch, gave them ketchup hair, snuck a pocket of danish out for later. She never put her cool hands to your cheek or asked the bad questions.

Once a man took you home to show you how his copy of *House of Leaves* was really a love story. There was blood on his white oxford shirt, your blood fixing hair down to his legs. He said: *It's cute.*

One day, you thought, *I will be a big van bartering snow. My body, a chilled beautiful blue. Eliza shifting a metal scrape of gears. Town to town, shake out wares like lived-on carpet in a stairwell. The place with all the men who fucked me will be desperate for some slush, gray as the fur on my back, freckled with pine, squirrel tail. When they reach to their pockets: pack up, hot tire, screech off. Tell them:* Under this skin, more skin

Why is there a delicious doe under all these poems, so sweet and glowing, like the blue fire of a dead star too far away to even fathom, gorgeous as a knife sponged into sugar-dusted yellow cake?

Once after ● raped you, he did not call for three days so you left a litany of messages brimming with apology.

Sometimes I am so scared. I think if I were to be raped again at least it would have the suggestion of an ending.

Once ● hit you so hard you could not hear for hours and when he asked why he did it, you knew.

I am an accumulation of *Once*; I refuse to look away.

● had this fantasy where I was with someone else, he'd kill them, lots of blood, then rape me in revenge—for what? For touch?

There are so many things I could touch and my hands are this big, still growing.

But I laid out on campus   concrete and ash
anointed bare back   But it was the August heat
thunder   But I don't want this
to just be   ● held me
by the corners of my mouth   made me
a fucked-up smile   But I wanted it   But
I was August heat thunder
I wanted it   I told him
I wanted it   But I walked to the gas station
for something to fry up   I told
him I wanted that   But I wanted   But I
wanted him to prop
the door open

Once ● tied your arms and legs to your throat, demanded you crawl because he made you immobile. I think a person can be there without being there.

You used to cry so much, wiped snot and kohl tears on the skirts of little dresses. It's overwrought to say, but true.

Can I make you sorry? Make you say you would be better if you knew what I know now?

What do I even know now—I am full of fear.

I was once a hand that went from overripe berry to next; a knife that cut nothing thicker than cake.

Say you were bloated with a place. Say you used to kick rock salt, rush from beds.

Prime for echo, shouting into the cleft of two walls.

And as for apology—say it. Say it. I want to hear you fucking say it.

It is not possible to function, to learn, to connect, to make progress, or even to hear in a climate of fear...Fear can be spotted like gold in the ground. Dig them out, and make them help you. Fears make the world go round.

LOUISE BOURGEOIS

One summer I bought a plant at the farmers market. When I took the money from my bra, the man smirked at me. I most likely killed it.

A climate of fear is both counting cards and laying its hand on the table.

There was a debate on campus about the semantics of *No means no*. Two philosophy professors in the key under a sagging hoop. Most of the women left before the Q & A.

Outside the department in the smoking pen, a man chastised his friend: *It's not bitches, they're females.*

Something grown: a sickness hollowing.

I heard: to pledge, a girl had to hold a carrot in her vagina. Tuft of greenish mud leaf.

The bus driver let the girl with no money on, then told her she'd have better luck lying in the bed of a pickup truck.

The jangling of an empty ambulance—the only concern with the driver is a matter of heroics.

At orientation they told us to go prone if a man put his hands on us. ● laughed because he knew.

Thought, *If it doesn't happen to me that's okay.*

I used to want the punchline at the beginning of the joke.

I used to fold paper into boats, and the story that followed had to do with sinking.

I had so much I wanted to say it feels like I've forgotten it all. It's TV static or a white noise machine. It's still a seen thing. It's still noise.

Little mouse, it's hard to tell if you're fearful, of what, and if it's your fear to be had.

I see you shake, but is that your blood or the way my eyes are darting?

The other day my friend spoke beautifully on gold. I forget now and it's just right beside me.

On the bus, after he touched me, the man moved his hand to my arm, gently, sincerely, said: *I am so sorry*.

/

I want to sling through the pastel of outreaching leaves, to fill a sugared bucket: I am not the little berries, I am not the bucket—I'm at the shovel; press loose dirt and lay the smooth blade aside. Oil away handle; for metal to rub off bit by bit—to be an expert at missing. I should be sorry. You know, there's no big finale or great reveal. No paw marked out in dust or carnage of purple husk. Can you not recognize how grotesque prey is up close? All gristle, all sweat—its blood pools from center, out.

/

I used to think I needed to instruct you. As if I had been a little mouse who needed teaching. Sweet mouse, you will not ask what makes a predator; there is something shadowed after you. It's less in the corners with metal snaps and more at the tip of your long and wonderful whiskers—and often it has whiskers too.

At the end of any fable a mouse, victorious. I'm not sure how to maneuver that moral, little sweet.

A predator as recognized by a growling—no: like a heater in the next room humming, that sounds like red herring. Predator when the knife is in hand—yes and also how it's raised, even just briefly, pressed, without breaking, to moving flesh. Knife when the predator is at hand—once the body of a man was always a sharp edge. Not anymore. The ones that still come to a point, I'm realizing, are made clear, so bright, like metal, all metal, just glint in the sun.

/

In the bad dream the man on the bus keeps sleeping on me.

In the bad dream the boys hold me down but don't grab me.

In the bad dream I'm disappointed when a friend saves me and we set ●'s house on fire.

In the bad dream all of my friends turn like the bad has been inside them all along.

In the bad dream I set the house on fire and don't think twice.

/

It's cold to kiss the girl in the mirror. I forget all the time (though it's true) that the mouse is the most successful mammal on the planet. I think victory and survival unruly bedfellows. I think if I were to maneuver an intricate burrow, it would be more than an architectural feat.

Okay, the woman in any fable or tale. Sure, a man traps her—but how she got in bed relies on a sniff for meat in her own psyche, or so I read. When she takes the key to the forbidden room and finds the broken-down yellow mess of woman bones, blood pours and pours from the key, it would fill her if she swallowed it. What doesn't fit is hard to think about.

Mouse, but not a mouse—wolf cub learning. Soft belly.

At Geneseo, in a little book tucked beneath a mattress, I wrote letters to myself: "I dream / my name is a carousel— / he takes a turn— / I don't spin / (or stay still): I watch lips / widen with the sea—

he built for her a duplicate of earth,
everything the same, down to the meadow,
but with a bed added.
LOUISE GLÜCK

Geneseo, NY

He was doing that thing today where he looks up other colleges' programs to laugh at their courses. Another gem from the trip: "Boat shoes were made for curb stomping." &, "The only thing that blows my mind is existentialism —also puppies." He's so ridiculous. I left, mascara on his pillow all wet. Forgot a pair of underwear on purpose.

Whenever I'm in the car, I sing like he's buckled in next to me. I order burgers from the window as if they're for the two of us. I fall asleep on my right side, his arms a weight I could never forget.

Soon,

Geneseo, NY

Yesterday he said to me, "Of course I love you, you're my
Lucia." I don't mean to be a portrait of a romantic
knowing parts, but there were things done to him he can't
even say.

Do you remember just before New Years, when you sat on
the carpet behind his bench & the first thing he did was
open the music to the symphony you loved: "Shh I'm
doing art now."

Soon,

Geneseo, NY

When he cried at the end of *Good Will Hunting* I put my hand on his leg & he let me touch him.

I keep writing these instructional poems, like "Lilac my cheeks from the inside, smell / your loud onion-heart renaming my tongue and palms."

I'm like the dove on the lawn signs by our old church: "I Leave Peaceprints." The room covered in molted feathers & white shit, a bright cooing of love, love, love.

Soon,

Geneseo, NY

I feel so little, so small with him & I love it. It's like when
Faulkner wrote, "The shape of my body where I used to be
a virgin is in the shape of a   ." I'm a sweet thing of foamed
milk forgotten on his lips. I want to kick holes in the brick
pressed to my dorm bed & climb in—can you believe how
much asbestos they let creep & crawl in these walls?

Soon,

Geneseo, NY

He says my love grows from a big space to an even bigger one.

This is what happens when you're sure: it's fear full of loss. I'm standing at the ledge & he is a balloon I'm afraid to drop—totally ignorant that he would just float, a perfect pressure—just in front of my face—so close I could smell the latex.

One day you'll see that these letters are full of love for you too & there will be so much you'll want to suck out of them, like pomegranate, juice & seeds six in your palm.

Soon,

Geneseo, NY

I went & saw that girl from high school in her dorm across
campus. She was like, "Damn, Lucia" when I did some of
the Nicki part of "Roman's Revenge" probably because she
thinks I'm a virgin. Last week, he finally did it with me. On
the basement carpet, which was rough & gave me a crazy
brush burn. In the ghazal, I wrote: "The body regenerates
at such a pace, curdling reminders until / it tries to forget for
you. Shed, layer, tighten—" but I hope the scab on my back,
big & purple as a plum, scars.

Soon,

Geneseo, NY

He puts his arm around me, in the dream, says, "I want to
take a picture." In the dream, for once he's warm on my
shoulder & not waiting in the wings. In the dream, we are in
the bow of a ship on a third floor. In the dream, we
sleep where the bed blows the walls open—plaster balloon.
In the dream, he steadies himself at our windowpane lined
with postcards. In the dream, I wake with the taste of irises.
Breakfast. Yellow soap. Coffee. No more cream, just cartons.

Soon,

Geneseo, NY

If his heart is an autoclave, I am a startle of bacteria buzzing
inside of it. I just learned that—some bacteria thrive in the
cataclysmic pressure of steam & heat.

I'm writing these missals because I want you to look
around & recognize the fiery & gorgeous that survived.
One day you'll write a beautiful book; the love you feel for
him will be a palimpsest of joy—: the flurry of last notes he
keys, then the jump, from the piano bench, onto you.

Soon,

Small death   Small shame
Photograph of a small room
emptied   Portrait of
women killing Orpheus   body
small in death   in pieces
I did not find pleasure in that
A small death   Do you feel shame
when you are dead   something always
lives on   small
When you are dead know this hand
is yours   no one comes to claim it
Told me a rape   is a small
death   something still lives
a blasphemous love   for myself
and not dead   or small   There
is nothing triumphant
about red rising   like next day

After ●, I knew a man with a loud voice and I couldn't stand it. A vibration like a cartoon halo zigzagging my body. I was bothered. I was a bother.

The murder was national news. You can understand that. Viral, like a virus, like violence as contagious, patient zero from one location.

Before, the most viral thing from Geneseo was a sunset, fluid and silhouette-making.

Shock triggers some endorphin, I'm sure. How surprise is a joy. What bothers me is never testimony, but the vertical scroll of all caps.

[Status Update Upstate]

Obviously you've never seen Fatal Attraction. You ladies should protest by not shaving your armpits. Go screw yourself. I will protect everyone I can. Idiot feminist. #awfulnews. 😵 A place I call home. My sisterhood is a few houses down. Sheesh. So sad to see this happen, especially Geneseo. Actually, there's already a lot of deaths. Actually, he was a really nice kid. Actually, I'm surprised they even did a story about this.

The novelist writes, *There is no good language when it comes to the unspeakable.* Instead, I write truly bad poems about the husk of my insides fallen out.

My friend gently rearranges commas, asks me to consider the Bachelard, then *Dictée*. She tells me to burn then bury it. It's taken so long to get to magic. I wasn't even desperate then.

In the bad dream I walk to the room and sit behind a desk, nothing shifts or is altered, furthest reaches of imagination falter.

Once I took the photographs, I sent them to ●.

Then, untied myself, got up off the floor.

My friend and I got drunk and switched clothes, a fold of dark liquid, mirror of once-very-charming. She repeats, *The most interesting moment is in a crease, the joint of the thing bent.*

My friend, she saw me as a thing in her lap, and she was warm, and I knew I was close. Like a jerking fish tries to pull oxygen from air.

Shaky voice, a little machine—we both know a method you cannot duplicate. If I hang up a phone to cry, it doesn't matter and I try at a tear.

Once I sat in an atrium while a man tuned a piano. The notes were not discordant, but patiently organized into melody.

My mother told me that I hate men.

I loved a man and he was kind to me. That was not a mistake.

When I look up *distraught*, the examples babble on about women hysterical, screaming. Online, all these sentences with a man so distraught he kills a woman, one he loved, one who was kind, and her voice, or mine, a crackled throat.

[Status Update Upstate]

There are around 7 billion other humans on this earth, so I believe you have many other opportunities at love. There was a third Geneseo student, I don't know what he was going through. I have been touched by the ripple of tragedy. Remember. 🙏 So sad. I'm sad. 🪦 Thoughts and prayers. My corner of the world needs LOVE. Does yours?

So I listened to a lot of the Mountain Goats, so I still listen to "Rhapsody in Blue," so I had a poster of John Lennon. So I moved dorms because my roommate loved to masturbate, so I loved to masturbate. So I didn't recognize it when he raped me. So I was raped. So I had a rape done to me. So I wrote about blood and onion hearts and beautiful bruises. So he dumped me on Skype.

Once I tweeted ways a woman is a slut, once I listed how a woman did things to herself. When I say once, I mean many times. I was a bad student and artless with irony.

After ● but before now. What happens in a beginning. I was there but I don't remember. I was there but that's not the woman I want. I'm a bad student. I can't show my work. I was there. I was there. I know her.

I stayed in Geneseo for another year. I moved away. I talked about ●. I talked about him a lot.

Once I thought if I were to drown I would pull him down with me, but the only hand in mine is mine.

It's funny: memory can be such a flash bang, shock of recognize (crack of knuckles reaching for a bunch of grapes, rough slats covering a mailbox, squishy air freshener in a Rite Aid bright light).

When I think of ● and how he did the bad things it's never on purpose or even in the same way. It feels like I'm repeating myself because I am repeating myself.

I saw two people coming down the sidewalk towards me, the man walking backwards while facing the woman. When they turned, I saw there was a large thing carried between them.

A man in his car trying to get to the cemetery called me a cunt through both windows. (I was still cold with ice cream, outside the parlor an older couple helped each other up the stairs. *That looks good*, a man had said.) A month ago I read a book that called me a cunt. When I was sixteen a man followed me into a supermarket to call me a cunt (a couple times). In a class a man referenced my cunt as if it were headgear. Yesterday my sister told me I am *a fucking cunt with huge anger issues.*

I'm jealous of anger.

I keep dreaming of cars without brakes and somehow I'm still full of apology. I keep dreaming I go to punch a face and my hand is a weak caress. I want to be ● when he couldn't get the bartender's attention. I want to throw the menu, shout, kick things, shake a person by the shoulders, and not have the person be me.

If I could reach into the past, would I snuff it out? I fell in love with another man. He wakes from a dream in which a man puts out a cigarette on my back. Then, in the dream, he leaves to, quote, *beat the life out of the guy*. This shouldn't surprise me. Once a coworker said he would punch ● if only I would tell him where. That a man might dip his tries in honey. What could be made sweet and smooth like a serrated blade on cut-proof gloves.

If it were my dream I would be the man's pinched forefinger and thumb, the perfect circle burn, and I'd never see my face. My mother had a bad dream. When I ask her to tell it to me, all she says is: *It was bad, bad, just bad.*

The mouth opens like it's just blunt entry.

I want to have sex with what I want to become, says the poet.

I think I should feel very broken down, very rotten. But I am open like the hull of a ship with stairs ascending. When I see a grease fire, it's a trash fire, it's a car engine fire, it's on the belly of a great lake.

I'm always looking for solution, but an equation would be too elegant. Siri says, *Thank you for your feedback* when you call her *naughty girl.* I know I shouldn't be filling any cup to splash. When I say grease fire, I mean nothing else. I mean grease fire.

I tell my lover to throw me onto the bed and he refuses. What happens when you are hot with the bad things?

When I was younger, I felt a tenderness that was uninterrupted. Now when I feel it coming on, I think I know where it started.

When I open I need to know who. Or, when my mouth opens, it's full of fire and still so hungry.

As a child, one of my friends loved the girl. Years after the murder, she posts in memory of. It's beautiful. Back of the photo, a dad in a Geneseo sweatshirt, bright light filters prophetic. I don't know which girl is which.

A man I know posted a documentary about any campus, #rewatching.

When I watched that film I was so mad—I already knew everything they told me. Who was that for? Who are these poems for? A hashtag has an edge. Lead me out red exit neon when the tacit applause comes.

There are so many things ● did to me and I don't want to just say.

My small small self. My little warm nub. I see your dead body everywhere flat on cement—spread-eagle and pulled to a point where your paws should be. Sometimes waterlogged, and others black matted mud. It's still coming. It's still happening. Even when I step over you and look at the sky.

A little moss on the wall   How do I tell him   Every time
a man touches it's better with the promise of worse   I love
a man   How do I tell him   My mother says I don't
seem happy at all   He forgets
to lock the door at night   How do I tell him   A sweet mass
of something big that presses   *Life is amazing!* I say
when a friend asks   How do I
tell him   I'm kneeling
on a chair   wobble and sweat   *Life is*
amazing! I repeat louder   then louder   then louder
then louder   And believe it

● lives in California now, near our old friends. I pretend I don't already know when one tells me over drinks.

He asked about you—asked if he was allowed to ask—he said: "Is she doing good? I hope she's doing good."

His voice no longer a gas leak down a hallway, stovetop fume without spark.

The snow outside the window should stop, freeze midair, become a curtain to walk through.

I think he knows he was a pretentious ass back then. You can tell he feels awful about the way he was.

She adds, *He's more aware.*

I don't know how to use this information.

Even now, as I write, I have no direction for the curved line that touches him.

When other poets read this they suggest I take it out. It humanizes ●. But humans do terrible things, and they do them all the time.

Still, I bring a strange hand to my lip and say *this*.

I tell my friends we are so quick to forget pleasure, and then we bring up poems we hate. Hate is a kind of pleasure.

When people post the man and his large knife they mention, *This is how many hills I was from the unlocked back door*. There is an exquisite joy in climbing a hill. What can be blotted out? A man? A name? A life? I'm trying and nothing seems to be working. Is anything lost in memoriam with a tweet? Is connection a kind of joy? I am tired and still watching.

I want her alive; point to her, be able to see *this*. I want to find a younger me, tell her *this*. I want to write a poem that says *this*.

I had a dream of a memory and the memory was when I had died. Wouldn't you like to see who did what to me.

When I left podunk Geneseo, my friends were sad and expected I'd be sad too, but that's not what happened.

Here too an expectation of forgiveness.

I left for a new city, rusty, hemmed in with bridges. Where I live the bus doesn't stop unless you flag it down, marquees CHANGE IS COMING between street names. I want the orange words when I close my eyes couched in black. CHANGE IS COMING. Ominous leads to true. Zooms by.

I would like to witness change, a quick shift more monumental than crossing the street, a wave to where I once stood waiting.

Another shared article, collaged photographs that don't match: her, her lover, her, the murderer, the house. The house, grass peeked through snow, red garland forgotten, two people bundled; from the side they look so close together, legs in sync, like this one a woman and the other a shadow.

The bear on the fountain in the center of Geneseo like a pit in a peach. Like the stomach of a body. A truck hit it last winter. Then another a month later. And again last week.

When I go back, it won't be there. It'll be like I'm not going back at all.

A silly hope.

As if everything that ever happens in a place has an edge like an aerial shot of it.

That memory could be stilled then framed, like a penned-up animal.

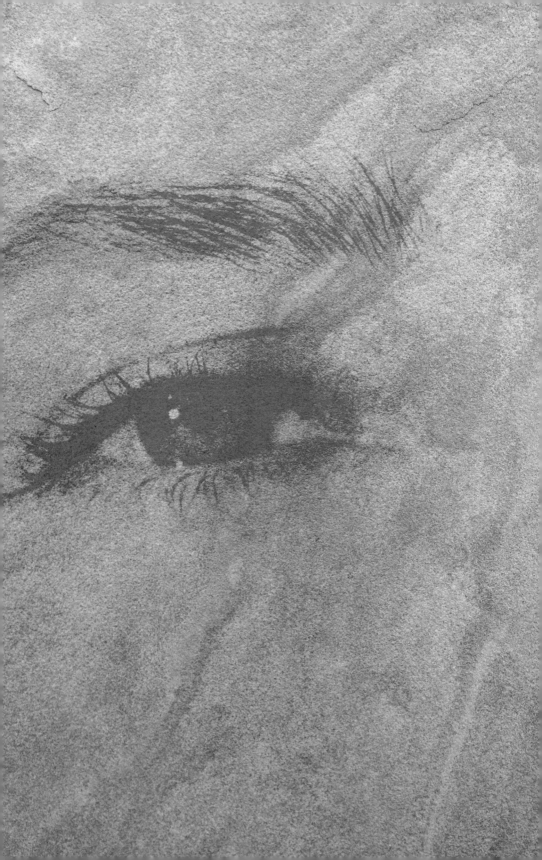

NOTES

This book's first epigraph is from Beth Bachmann's poem "Colorization" from her collection *Temper*, and the second is from Anne Carson's *Nox*.

The "[Status Update Upstate]" pieces are made up of language culled from January 2016 posts and comments on Facebook about Geneseo.

The epigraph from Louise Bourgeois was found in *Destruction of the Father, Reconstruction of the Father: Writings and Interviews, 1923-1997*.

The epigraph written by Louise Glück is from her poem "A Myth of Devotion" from her collection *Averno*.

The text alluded to on page 31 is *Women Who Run with the Wolves: Myths and Stories of the Wild Woman Archetype* by Clarissa Pinkola Estés.

The William Faulkner quotation on page 42 is from *As I Lay Dying*.

The novelist cited on page 52 is Yiyun Li, quoted from her book *Where Reasons End*.

The poet cited on page 64 is Bhanu Kapil, quoted from her book *Incubation: A Space for Monsters*.

Though she is never cited or mentioned, much of this book was written while thinking about Maggie Nelson's *The Art of Cruelty: A Reckoning* and *Jane: A Murder*, and drafts included epigraphs from these two texts.

Please consider supporting your local domestic violence support organizations with time or money. I urge you to donate to the Kelsey A. Annese Memorial Scholarship fund, which can be found through the SUNY Geneseo website.

ACKNOWLEDGMENTS

I have earnest gratitude for those who have guided and supported and shepherded and moved to understand me—I'm glad to share it here.

Thank you to *Passages North* and to *Pinwheel* for publishing excerpted and slightly changed sequences from this book. Thank you to KMA Sullivan for naming this book a finalist for two YesYes Books series and offering thoughtful feedback. Thank you to the staff and readers at the National Poetry Series for including this book as a finalist in their annual open competition.

Thank you to the keen editorial team at Alice James Books—Alyssa Neptune, Julia Bouwsma, and Emily Marquis. Thank you Carey Salerno, for this life-altering pluck out of nothingness, for seeing me and seeing this book.

Cori A. Winrock, this book would not be possible without you, nor would I be a poet. Thank you for your galactic mind and unwarranted support. For the hardsugar, the glitterfizz—for helping me find how to "clamp the heart like a caught wrist."

Suzannah Russ Spaar, without you I would not survive, nor could I have imagined beyond the small parcel of what I thought was possible in art, in collaboration, in poetics, in truth, in friendship, in tenderness, in the acts of loving oneself. Thank you, and thank you.

Thank you Dawn Lundy Martin for seeing what my work was reaching for before I was even close to grasping it. Thank you for your brilliance and your method.

Yona Harvey, thank you for the space, the difficult questions, for guiding me to echo, for not allowing me to undermine myself.

Thank you Lauren Russell—for rigor, for difficulty, for precision, for, with scissors and tape, helping me find a way out.

Angie Cruz—your mentorship is without match. Thank you for leading me to be a more thoughtful and tenacious writer and advocate.

Thank you to this constellation of radiant poets: Stephanie Cawley, S. Brook Corfman, Gabrielle Ralambo-Rajerison, and Steffan Triplett. Your approaches to poetics and genre are transformative. You are all so giving, so important to me, and so much better.

For nuance and for exploration, thank you to all of my teachers and mentors, including Caroline Beltz-Hosek, Fiona Cheong, Lynn Emanuel, Piotr Gwiazda, Rachel Hall, Terrance Hayes, Jenny Johnson, Maria Helena Lima, Neepa Majumdar, Ellen McGrath Smith, and Lytton Smith.

Thank you to the intersecting cohorts of writers at the University of Pittsburgh who came to me and my work with generosity. Particular gratitude to Hannah Eko for meditative magic and strength. And to Kathryn Waring, when it was all over, for unlocking the in-between of this book.

Caile Collins—thank you for listening and for being there.

For letters, eggs, revolving em-dashed colons, and first bright sparks, thank you to Erin Kae, Devin Conde, Joey O'Connor, Anna Kushnir, and especially Amy Elizabeth Bishop, who read stumbling first drafts.

Thank you Devon Gawley for being my friend, for understanding me.

To my family—thank you for love, thank you for resilience, thank you for ferocity, thank you for feeling.

To repeat one grateful incantation—to Suzannah, because my gratitude is bigger than the page, but for now the page is all I have.

And finally, importantly, Matt Griffin. Sweet Matt. Thank you for the Year of Lucia, speaking this all into fruition. For your generous heart. For your world-building goof. The unwavering support you give is more than I ever anticipated from a partner. And your love—it overwhelms. Thank you. I love you.

RECENT TITLES
FROM ALICE JAMES BOOKS

Alice James Books is committed to publishing books that matter. The press was founded in 1973 in Boston, Massachusetts as a cooperative, wherein authors performed the day-to-day undertakings of the press. This element remains present today, as authors who publish with the press are invited to collaborate closely in the publication process of their work. AJB remains committed to its founders' original feminist mission, while expanding upon the scope to include all voices and poets who might otherwise go unheard. In keeping with its efforts to build equity and increase inclusivity in publishing and the literary arts, AJB seeks out poets whose writing possesses the range, depth, and ability to cultivate empathy in our world and to dynamically push against silence. The press was named for Alice James, sister to William and Henry, whose extraordinary gift for writing went unrecognized during her lifetime.

Designed by Tiani Kennedy

Printed by McNaughton & Gunn